The Story of "THE STAR-SPANGLED BANNER"

Lori Damanda

The Rosen Publishing Group's
PowerKids Press™
New York

Published in 2009 by The Rosen Publishing Group, Inc.
29 East 21st Street, New York, NY 10010

Book Design: Daniel Hosek

Photo Credits: Cover, pp. 20–21, 22–23, 28 (top) © Bettmann/Corbis; p. 4 © Dirk Anschutz/Stone/Getty Images; p. 5 © John Munson/Star Ledger/Corbis; p. 6 courtesy Maryland State Archives; pp. 7, 12 (bottom), 24 (top) courtesy Wikimedia Commons; p. 9 © Peter Harholdt/Corbis; p. 10 © The Gallery Collection/Corbis; p. 11 © Adam Woolfitt/Corbis; p. 12 (top) © National Archives/Getty Images; p. 14 © James Brereton/ The Bridgeman Art Library/Getty Images; pp. 17, 26, 27 courtesy Library of Congress Prints and Photographs Division; p. 18 © Paul A. Souders/Corbis; p. 19 Military History, Smithsonian Institution; p. 24 (bottom) © Massimo Listri/Corbis; p. 25 © Hulton Archive/Getty Images; p. 28 (bottom) © Corbis.

Library of Congress Cataloging-in-Publication Data

Damanda, Lori.
  The story of the "Star-spangled banner" / Lori Damanda.
      p. cm.
  Includes index.
  ISBN 978-1-4358-0205-6 (pbk.)
  6-pack ISBN 978-1-4358-0206-3
  ISBN 978-1-4358-3015-8 (lib. bdg.)
  1. Baltimore, Battle of, Baltimore, Md., 1814—Juvenile literature. 2. Star Spangled Banner (Song)—Juvenile literature. 3. National songs—United States—History and criticism—Juvenile literature. 4. Key, Francis Scott, 1779-1843—Juvenile literature. 5. Flags—United States—History—19th century—Juvenile literature. 6. American poetry—History and criticism—Juvenile literature. I. Title.
  E83.67D36 2009
  782.42'15990973-dc22

                          2008047092

Manufactured in the United States of America

INDEX

OH SAY CAN YOU SEE...

Most students in the United States say the Pledge of **Allegiance** in front of the American flag at the beginning of each school day. What are we doing when we say the pledge? Why do we keep this tradition? We do it to honor our country—the United States of America.

Before many sporting events, players and fans stand and listen to a song. This song is our **national anthem**, and it's called "The Star-**Spangled** Banner." Do you know why this song is played at special moments and sporting events? Just like the pledge, it honors the United States. It's a symbol of the love and respect we have for our country.

The words to "The Star-Spangled Banner" were written in 1814 by an American lawyer named Francis Scott Key. This book tells the story of the historic events Key witnessed that inspired him to write what became one of the country's most meaningful songs.

Fans and players honor the United States by standing and singing "The Star-Spangled Banner" before the seventy-ninth Major League Baseball All-Star Game.

Francis Scott Key was born to a wealthy family in Frederick County, Maryland, around 1780. The United States was a new nation at that time. His father, John Ross Key, had been an officer during the American Revolution. He was also a lawyer and a judge. Francis Scott Key had five **siblings**, although three died before reaching adulthood. The Key family lived on a large estate called Terra Rubra, which is Latin for "red earth."

Key's parents taught him school subjects at home until he was 10. Then he went to a school in Annapolis, Maryland. When Key was

Francis Scott Key

17, he attended St. John's College in Annapolis. After graduating, Key went to work in the law office of his uncle, Phillip Barton Key, in order to study law.

Lawyer, Father, Poet

Key married Mary Tayloe Lloyd in 1802. In 1804, they moved to Georgetown, Maryland. Soon after, Key opened a law office near Washington, D.C. The Keys had eleven children and lived in Georgetown from 1804 until

"TERRA RUBRA"

THE BIRTHPLACE OF
FRANCIS SCOTT KEY
THE AUTHOR OF OUR
NATIONAL ANTHEM
"THE STAR-SPANGLED BANNER"

MARYLAND HISTORICAL SOCIETY

around 1833. Key was a deeply religious man and even considered leaving his law practice to become a preacher. Although Key lived a busy life as a husband, father, and lawyer, he liked reading poetry. He also enjoyed writing poetry in his spare time. His most famous poem, written during the War of 1812, is today known as "The Star-Spangled Banner."

Key became a major figure in Georgetown society and U.S. politics. His law practice was very successful. He even argued some cases at the highest court in the nation, the U.S. **Supreme Court**. Later, in 1833, President Andrew Jackson appointed Key to be U.S. district **attorney** of Washington, D.C. Key died in 1843. Today he is remembered as the author of "The Star-Spangled Banner" and an American patriot. Let's look back at Key's role in the War of 1812 and how it inspired him to write our national anthem.

What Is a District Attorney?

A district attorney, or D.A., is a lawyer appointed to office by a local, state, or federal government. The D.A. represents the government during criminal trials. U.S. district attorneys—also called federal **prosecutors**—represent the federal government in courts all over the country. Today, there are ninety-three U.S. district attorneys serving under the Attorney General, who is the head of the U.S. Department of Justice.

John Marshall, shown here, was Chief Justice of the U.S. Supreme Court from 1801 to 1835, the time during which Key was practicing law in Washington, D.C.

THE WAR OF 1812

Beginning in 1793, Britain and France often waged war with each other. The leader of France, an emperor named Napoleon Bonaparte, wanted to conquer Britain, but the British were too powerful. Napoleon instead hoped to disrupt British trade with other nations by preventing British ships from entering ports under French control. In turn, Britain issued orders that required foreign ships to stop in Britain

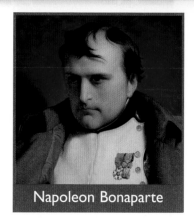

Napoleon Bonaparte

before going to France. The ships were then loaded with British goods. These actions had a negative effect on the United States, which had been getting rich from trade with European countries.

In the early 1800s, the powerful British navy controlled the seas. Many British sailors had **deserted** the British navy to work on U.S. trading ships. British ships often stopped U.S. ships and took the British sailors, but they began **kidnapping** hundreds of American sailors, too. The sailors were forced to work for the British navy. These actions angered many people in the United States. The U.S. government passed a series of trade laws in an effort to punish the British, but most failed.

Britain Invades

The United States and Britain continued to argue over trade issues. On June 18, 1812, the United States used the kidnapping of American citizens and the disruption of U.S. trade as reasons to declare war against Britain. During

The H.M.S. Victory, shown here, is a British ship that participated in many battles against the French between 1778 and 1812.

1812 and 1813, the United States attacked British land in Canada. In August 1814, the British attacked Washington, D.C. They burned the White House and the U.S. Capitol. President James Madison and members of Congress had to escape Washington, D.C., quickly when the British arrived.

James Madison

During this time, Francis Scott Key was a lawyer living with his family in Georgetown, Maryland. He was very much against war, but he was a devoted patriot. Key joined the U.S. army to help defend his country. In 1813, he served for a short time in a Maryland **militia**.

Save the President!

In 1814—as British forces invaded Washington, D.C.—First Lady Dolly Madison hurried to save several objects before fleeing the White House with President Madison. One was this portrait of President George Washington, which was painted by Gilbert Stuart in 1796. Today, this portrait hangs at the National Portrait Gallery of the Smithsonian Institution in Washington, D.C. A copy of the painting is on display in the East Room of the White House.

The War of 1812

Britain and France had been at war periodically since 1793.

↓

Britain and France set up **blockades** to disrupt each other's trade.

↓

The blockades hurt U.S. business with other countries.

↓

The British navy stopped U.S. trading ships, took British deserters, and kidnapped American sailors.

↓

British actions angered many people in the United States.

↓

The U.S. government passed a series of trade laws in an effort to punish the British.

↓

The United States used the kidnapping of American citizens and the disruption of U.S. trade as reasons to declare war against Britain.

DR. WILLIAM BEANES

After the British burned Washington, D.C., they moved northeast to attack the important harbor at Baltimore, Maryland. On the way, three British soldiers who were traveling alone stopped at the home of Dr. William Beanes, who was a friend of Francis Scott Key. The soldiers were looking for food,

This painting of the *Tonnant* was created by English artist James Brereton.

shelter, and things to steal. Beanes and others who were at his home helped to arrest the soldiers and lock them in a local jail. However, other British soldiers arrived and arrested Beanes.

A **fleet** of British ships that had gathered in Chesapeake Bay was preparing to attack Baltimore. Dr. Beanes was taken to General Robert Ross and Admiral Alexander Cochrane on the British ship the *Tonnant*. Ross himself had used Beanes's farm as a headquarters during a recent battle in Bladensburg, Maryland. Upon hearing of Beanes's actions, Ross decided he had to be punished. The people of Maryland were afraid that Beanes would be **executed**. Something had to be done quickly to save the doctor's life.

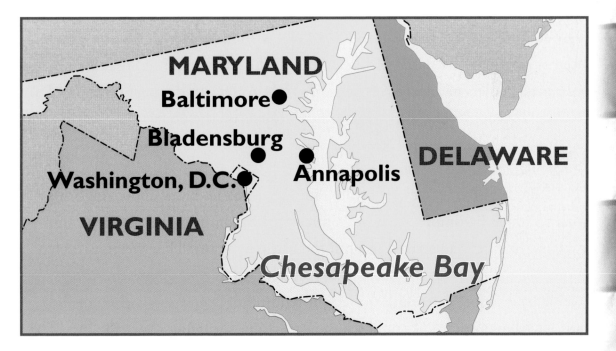

THE RESCUE OF DR. BEANES

Upon hearing about the arrest of Dr. Beanes, Key knew he had to help his friend. Key went to President Madison with a plan to rescue Beanes. With the president's approval, Key traveled to Baltimore, where he met with Colonel John Skinner. Skinner was an American agent who arranged for prisoner exchanges with the enemy. On September 3, 1814, Key and Skinner set out from Baltimore on a ship flying a flag of truce, which showed they were coming for a peaceful purpose. On September 7, they arrived at the *Tonnant*.

Key and Skinner were welcomed aboard the British warship. Admiral Cochrane invited the men to his cabin and discussed Dr. Beanes with them. They pleaded for the doctor's release. At first, the officers refused and insisted that Beanes had to be punished for his actions. However, Key and Skinner showed Ross and Cochrane a stack of letters written by British soldiers who had been wounded at the Battle of Bladensburg. The letters reported that the wounded soldiers had received good care from American doctors, including Dr. Beanes. This convinced the British officers to release the doctor.

Not So Fast . . .

By this time, however, Key, Skinner, and Beanes knew about the British plan to attack Baltimore. They were forced to remain on board the small ship Key and Skinner had arrived in until the battle was over. They were instructed to anchor their boat at the back of the British fleet as they approached Fort McHenry, the fort defending the city of Baltimore. Even from a distance, Key and his fellow Americans could see the American flag flying above the fort. The

This is an artist's interpretation of Key aboard the small ship before the battle.

17

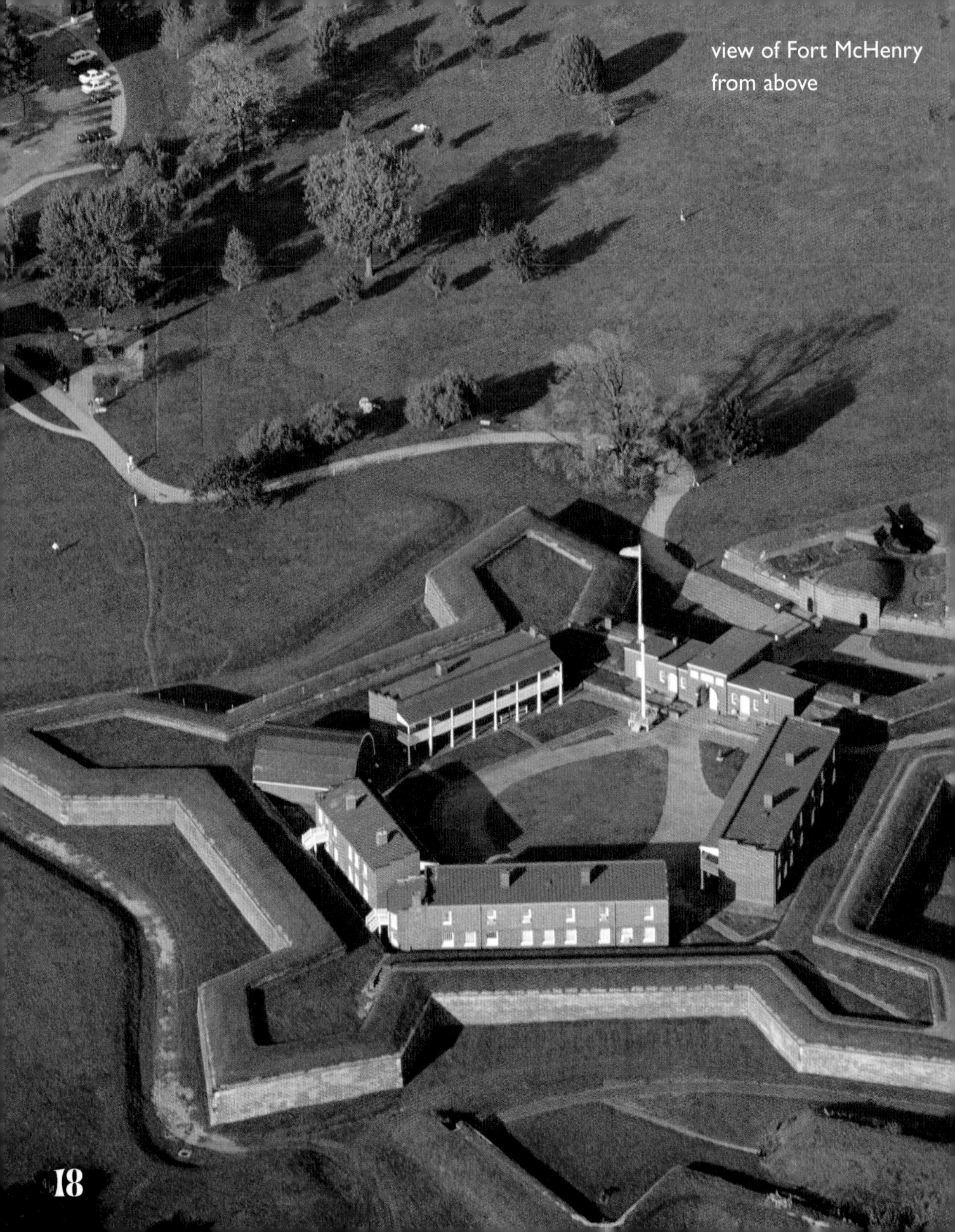

U.S. officer in charge of Fort McHenry, Major George Armistead, had the flag made large enough so the British could see it from a great distance. This was "the star-spangled banner" that inspired Key's poem.

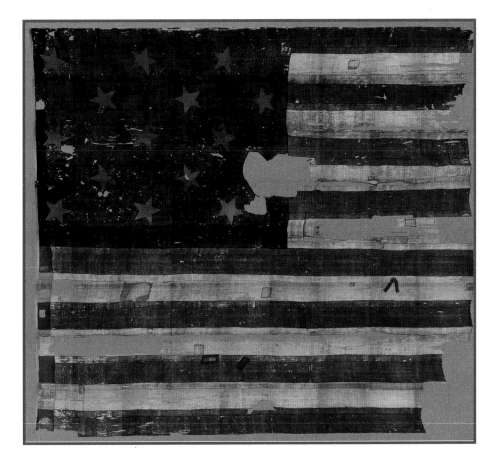

Shown here is the flag that Key saw flying over Fort McHenry.

THE BOMBS BURSTING IN AIR

On September 13, 1814, at about 7 A.M., the British fleet began attacking Fort McHenry. The British knew that if they could capture this fort, Baltimore could be beaten just as Washington, D.C., had been a few weeks earlier.

Key, Skinner, and Beanes looked on helplessly for 25 hours as the country they loved was attacked by the world's most powerful navy. The British fired

over 1,500 bombs at Fort McHenry. The bombs had fuses that were lit before they were fired, and many bombs exploded in the air before they reached the fort. The British also fired small rockets at the fort that made red trails in the air as they flew.

The American forces in Fort McHenry fought back bravely. They had intentionally sunk twenty-two American merchant ships near the fort, clogging

A View of the Bombardment of Fort McHenry shows "bombs bursting in air" during the attack.

the water with debris. The British ships weren't able to get close to the fort because of the sunken ships.

Our Flag Was Still There

Key, Skinner, and Beanes knew that as long as the bombs kept flying, the soldiers in Fort McHenry hadn't given up the fight. However, early on a dark and rainy September 14, shortly before sunrise, the sounds of war fell silent. The men wondered what it meant. Had the British won? They could do nothing but wait for dawn. It was a nervous time for the three patriots aboard their tiny ship.

Then, as dawn's early light rose, they looked across the water to see that the huge flag was still waving above Fort McHenry! This meant the Americans had won the battle. The British decided that the battle was becoming too costly to continue and had begun to retreat.

The moment was an emotional one for Key and his friends. Inspired by the patriotic scene, Key began to write a poem about the battle on the back of an envelope he had in his pocket. This was the beginning of "The Star-Spangled Banner."

Key and Skinner salute the American flag on September 14, 1814.

Once the British fleet had retreated, Key, Skinner, and Beanes sailed back to Baltimore. Key continued to write his poem that night in his hotel room. The next day, Key took the complete poem—titled "Defence of Fort McHenry"—to his brother-in-law, Judge Joseph H. Nicholson. Nicholson was so impressed with the poem that he immediately had copies of it printed up on **handbills** that were given to people around Baltimore. Less than a week later, the poem was published in the *Baltimore Patriot* newspaper. Soon after, it was published in newspapers from Georgia to New Hampshire. It quickly became a popular patriotic song for American citizens.

copy of handbill

From Poem to Song

Shortly after being published, Americans began to sing "Defence of Fort McHenry" to the tune of a popular song originally called "To Anacreon in Heaven." The song, about an ancient Greek poet named Anacreon, was written around 1770 and became popular in the United States and

statue of Anacreon

O say can you see by the dawn's early light
What so proudly we hail'd at the twilight's last gleaming,
Whose broad stripes & bright stars through the perilous fight
O'er the ramparts we watch'd, were so gallantly streaming?
    And the rocket's red glare, the bomb bursting in air,
    Gave proof through the night that our flag was still there
O say does that star-spangled banner yet wave
O'er the land of the free & the home of the brave?

On the shore dimly seen through the mists of the deep,
    Where the foe's haughty host in dread silence reposes,
What is that which the breeze, o'er the towering steep,
    As it fitfully blows half conceals half discloses?
    Now it catches the gleam of the morning's first beam,
    In full glory reflected now shines in the stream,
'Tis the star-spangled banner — O long may it wave
O'er the land of the free & the home of the brave!

And where is that band who so vauntingly swore,
    That the havoc of war & the battle's confusion
A home & a Country should leave us no more?
    Their blood has wash'd out their foul footsteps pollution
No refuge could save the hireling & slave
From the terror of flight or the gloom of the grave,
And the star-spangled banner in triumph doth wave
O'er the land of the free & the home of the brave.

O thus be it ever when freemen shall stand
    Between their lov'd home & the war's desolation!
Blest with vict'ry & peace may the heav'n rescued land
    Praise the power that hath made & preserv'd us a nation!
    Then conquer we must when our cause it is just,
    And this be our motto — "In God is our trust"
And the star-spangled banner in triumph shall wave
O'er the land of the free & the home of the brave.

some countries in Europe. It became such a popular melody that many songwriters wrote new **lyrics** to go with it.

Many people think that a Baltimore actor named Ferdinand Durang was the first to sing Key's lyrics in public to the tune of "To Anacreon in Heaven." A music publisher in Baltimore who printed Key's words together with the music was the first to use the title "The Star-Spangled Banner." The song became an instant success across the young nation and became even more popular when the War of 1812 ended in December 1814.

Set to Music

"To Anacreon in Heaven" was originally composed by a British musician named John Stafford Smith. The original words were written by another Englishman named Ralph Tomlinson. Both men were members of the Anacreontic Society in London.

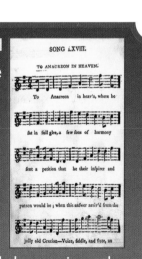

The music that Smith composed became very popular in England and America. It was used for dozens of songs, including patriotic songs such as "Jefferson and Liberty." It's likely that Key had heard the music, and that he had it in mind while writing his poem.

Throughout the 1800s, "The Star-Spangled Banner" continued to be a popular American song. It became an important symbol of the ideals Americans had come to embrace, particularly bravery and freedom. These same ideals were forever tied to the image of the star-spangled banner itself. The American flag and Key's dramatic story of the defense of Fort McHenry soon became inseparable symbols of American patriotism.

Woodrow Wilson

In 1916, President Woodrow Wilson ordered that the song be played during military and political ceremonies. Finally, on March 3, 1931, President Herbert Hoover signed a bill making "The Star-Spangled Banner" the national anthem of the United States. The tradition of playing the song before sporting events officially began during World War II. With their hands over their hearts, millions of Americans sing Key's words and salute their nation every day.

President Hoover (center) and his wife, Lou Henry Hoover, stand during "The Star-Spangled Banner."

Francis Scott Key's Life

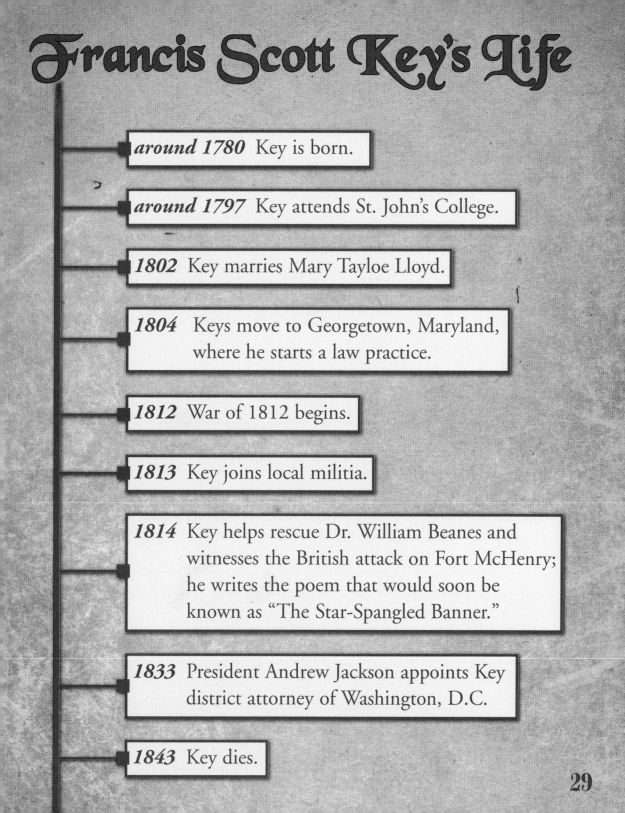

around 1780 Key is born.

around 1797 Key attends St. John's College.

1802 Key marries Mary Tayloe Lloyd.

1804 Keys move to Georgetown, Maryland, where he starts a law practice.

1812 War of 1812 begins.

1813 Key joins local militia.

1814 Key helps rescue Dr. William Beanes and witnesses the British attack on Fort McHenry; he writes the poem that would soon be known as "The Star-Spangled Banner."

1833 President Andrew Jackson appoints Key district attorney of Washington, D.C.

1843 Key dies.

"The Star-Spangled Banner" is a patriotic song, but it's also a beautiful poem. Like all good poets, Key worked hard to choose the perfect words for his poem. This chart shows the meanings of several key words in the poem, as well as synonyms for each word.

word	meaning	synonyms
proudly	marked by feelings of pride	with respect
hail'd	welcomed with a military greeting	saluted
perilous	full of danger	unsafe, risky
ramparts	protective walls around a fort	walls, fort
gallantly	bravely, grandly, and with great show	heroically, boldly, colorfully
spangled	decorated with small, bright shapes or colors	sprinkled, covered
banner	a piece of cloth displayed as a symbol of something	flag, national symbol
brave	people who show courage when facing danger	heroes, fearless people

Oh, say, can you see, by the dawn's early light,
What so proudly we hail'd at the twilight's last gleaming?
Whose broad stripes and bright stars, thru the perilous fight,
O'er the ramparts we watch'd, were so gallantly streaming?
And the rockets' red glare, the bombs bursting in air,
Gave proof thru the night that our flag was still there.
O say, does that star-spangled banner yet wave
O'er the land of the free and the home of the brave?

GLOSSARY

allegiance (uh-LEE-juhns) Loyalty to a country, group, or cause.

attorney (uh-TUHR-nee) A lawyer.

blockade (blah-KAYD) The use of ships to block entrance to or exit from an enemy country.

desert (dih-ZURT) To run away while serving in the military.

execute (EHK-sih-kyoot) To put to death.

fleet (FLEET) A number of warships acting as a single unit under the command of a single leader.

handbill (HAND-bihl) A small sheet of paper with information that is given to people by hand.

kidnap (KIHD-nap) To take somebody away by force and hold them prisoner.

lyrics (LIHR-ihks) The words to a song.

militia (muh-LIH-shuh) A group of people who are trained and ready to fight when needed.

national anthem (NA-shuh-nuhl AN-thum) A country's official song.

prosecutor (PRAH-sih-kyoo-tuhr) A lawyer for the government who charges people with crimes and takes them to court.

sibling (SIH-bling) A person's sister or brother.

spangled (SPAYN-guhld) Decorated with small, bright shapes or colors.

Supreme Court (suh-PREEM KORT) The highest court in the United States.

INDEX

Due to the changing nature of Internet links, The Rosen Publishing Group, Inc., has developed an online list of Web sites related to the subject of this book. This site is updated regularly. Please use this link to access the list: http://www.rcbmlinks.com/rlr/fskey